THE LITTLE BOOK OF HAPPINESS

SIMPLE WAYS TO BEAUTIFY YOUR LIFE

JAGAT SINGH BISHT

*This little book
is dedicated
to my son
ANURAG
who gives me
pure happiness,
nothing else.*

CONTENTS

INTRODUCTION

This book is about simple ways to beautify your life.

You can create your own happiness. It is hassle-free and you can do it yourself.

This book describes activities derived from the modern science of happiness as well as ancient spirituality, based on years of study and practical sessions with people.

You will learn about flow, work-happiness, mindfulness, laughter meditation, and happiness activities.

There are beautiful parables and inspirational quotes inside.

Experience new joy and freedom.

Are you ready?

On your marks.

Get set!

The journey of happiness begins...

HAPPINESS

Happiness is the experience of joy, contentment, or positive well-being, combined with a sense that one's life is good, meaningful, and worthwhile.

The best way to begin this journey of happiness would be with some inspiring quotes from truly happy people:

"If you want others to be happy, practice compassion. If you want to be happy, practice compassion."

-Dalai Lama

"Sometimes your joy is the source of your smile, but sometimes your smile can be the source of your joy."

-Thich Nhat Hanh

"All the joy the world contains,

Has come through wishing happiness for others.

All the misery the world contains,

Has come through wanting pleasure for oneself."

-Shantideva

"Real happiness comes from performing actions that contribute to the welfare of others by fulfilling responsibilities to family and society and performing actions that cleanse the mind."

-Buddha

"This is the true joy in life – being used for a purpose recognized by yourself as a mighty one."

-George Bernard Shaw

"Try to be a rainbow in someone's cloud."

-Maya Angelou

They only live who live for others.

-Swami Vivekananda

That is happiness – to be dissolved into something complete and great.

-Willa Cather

If you observe a really happy man, you will find him building a boat, writing a symphony, educating his son, growing double dahlias in his garden, or looking for dinosaur eggs in the Gobi Desert.

-Walter Beran Wolfe

"Friendship doubles joy and cuts grief in half. The number-one predictor of well-being is not money or prestige, not success or accolades, but rather the time we spend with people we care about and who care about us."

-Tal Ben-Shahar

"A good life is characterized by complete absorption in what one does."

-Jeanne Nakamura and Mihaly Csikszentmihalyi

THREE LAUGHING MONKS

We are progressing well in our journey of happiness.

Before we take the next step, let us savour a fascinating parable that is both – funny and inspiring.

The way Osho narrates it is mesmerizing:

"I have heard about three monks. No names are mentioned because they never disclosed their names to anybody. They never answered anything.

"In China, they are simply known as the three laughing monks. And they did only one thing: they would enter a village, stand in the marketplace, and start laughing.

"They would laugh with their whole being and suddenly people would become aware. Then others would also get the infection and a crowd would gather. The whole crowd would start laughing just because of them. What was happening? The whole town would get involved. Then they would move to another town.

"They were loved very much. That was their only sermon, their only message; that laugh. And they would not teach; they would simply create a situation.

"Then it happened that they became famous all over the country. Three laughing monks. All of China loved them, respected them. Nobody had ever preached in such a way that life must be just a laughter and nothing else.

"They were not laughing at anyone, in particular. They were simply laughing as if they had understood the Cosmic joke. And they spread so much joy all over China without using a single word. People would ask for their names, but they would simply laugh. So that became their name – the three laughing monks.

"Then they grew old. And while staying in one village. one of the three monks died. The whole village became very much expectant because they thought that when one of them had died, the other two would surely weep. This must be worth seeing because no one had ever seen these people weeping. The whole village gathered. But the two monks were standing beside the corpse of the third and laughing – such a belly laugh. So, the villagers asked them to explain this.

"So, for the first time, the two monks spoke and said, 'We are laughing because this man has won. We were always wondering as to who would die first and this man has defeated us. We are laughing at our defeat and his victory. Also, he lived with us for many years and we laughed together, and we enjoyed each other's togetherness, presence. There can be no better way of giving him the last send off. We can only laugh.

"But the whole village was sad. And when the dead monk's body was put on the funeral pyre, then the village realized that the remaining two monks were not the only ones who were joking, the third who was dead was also laughing. He had asked his companions not to change his clothes. It was conventional that when a man died, they changed his dress, and gave a bath to the body. So, the third monk had said, 'Don't give me a bath because I have never been unclean. So much laughter has been in my life that no impurity can accumulate, can come to me. I have not gathered any dust. Laughter is always young and fresh. So, don't give me a bath and don't change my clothes.'

"So, just to respect his wishes, they did not change his clothes. And when the body was put to fire, suddenly they became aware that he had hidden some Chinese fireworks under his clothes, and they had started going off. So, the whole village laughed, and the other two monks said: 'You rascal, you are dead, but you have defeated us once again. Your laughter is the last.'

"Then the whole village was laughing and dancing. Celebrating their life! Giving them a good send off - creating a Great Wave of ENERGY, LOVE, LIGHT! And these 3 monks could ride on this high wave of Energy! Everyone felt the Blessing of their life and their death. Love never dies, Laughter never dies, Life continues. As we CELEBRATE, everything is transformed into JOY and GRATEFULNESS!"

Deep gratitude, Osho, for sharing such a wonderful story.

ACTIVITY

Happiness consists in activity. It is like a flowing river, not a stagnant pool.

Agreed, all action may not bring happiness, but it is also true that there is no happiness without action.

So, get up, put on your walking shoes, and venture out for a long walk.

WALKING

If you want more happiness in your life, get up early and go for a brisk walk in the park nearby.

Go for a leisurely walk in the neighbourhood streets after you are back from work.

Go out for a long walk in the lap of nature on weekends.

Walking is soothing, relaxes your mind, and tones up your body.

EXERCISE

Everyone knows that exercise is good for the body, but do you know that exercise brings happiness. It is now scientifically confirmed.

Do freestyle exercises at home, on the terrace, or in the park. Stretch, bend, and twist your body freely. Rotate like the whirling dervishes.

Take time to breathe freely. Inhale and exhale deeply. Enjoy your moves. Relax. No tension of body and no tension of mind.

Just do whatever makes you happy.

YOGA

If you cannot find time for your daily yoga, there are exercises that take just ten minutes of your time, and you get all the benefits.

Surya namaskara, or salutation to the sun, is one such exercise. It is a series of twelve physical postures.

The alternating forward and backward bends flex and stretch the spinal columns and limbs through their maximum range.

Another, ancient practice comes from the Himalayas, and is known as the five rites of rejuvenation, or simply the Five Tibetans.

These five dynamic exercises enhance health, energy, and vitality.

They take only a minimum of daily time and effort, but dramatically increase flexibility of the body as well as mental sharpness.

DEEP BREATHING

The body needs oxygen for vitality. It is the life force.

Take three deep breaths whenever you find some time. It will refresh and relax you.

According to scientists, breathing correctly is the key to better fitness, muscle strength, stamina, and athletic endurance.

Oxygenation through deep breathing boosts the immune system and can rid the body of chronic illnesses.

You may also take up activities like, swimming, cycling, or jogging.

MINDFULNESS

The body needs activity, but the mind requires relaxation.

How do we tame the monkey mind? It is ever so distracted and restless. Like a monkey, it jumps from one branch of tree to another tirelessly.

The Buddha gave us a small practice for calming the mind that has been found to be of great benefit.

MINDFULNESS OF BREATHING

Early in the morning, spare a few minutes for yourself. Find a peaceful place and sit down comfortably.

Keep your back straight. Do not be stiff. Be relaxed. Close your eyes gently.

Settle down. No hurry. Listen to the sounds nearby and far away. Just listen. Do not worry.

When you are somewhat settled, bring your attention to the nostrils. Try to feel the incoming and outgoing breath.

If the breath is subtle and you are unable to feel it, take a few deep breaths.

Once you get a sense of the breath, leave it to flow naturally. Do not try to control it in any way.

Just observe.

Observe the breath as it goes in and as it comes out. Be mindful as you watch the incoming breath and the outgoing breath.

Like a watchman, keep a vigil on each breath. No breath should go in without your knowledge and no breath should come out without your scrutiny.

Be mindful, as you breathe in, and as you breathe out.

Keeping your eyes closed, look at your whole body from the top to the bottom. Pass your attention slowly from one part of the body to the other. Do not skip any part of the body.

All the while be mindful of the incoming and outgoing breath.

Relax your body as you breathe in and as you breathe out.

Ever mindful, breathe in, and breathe out.

Slowly open your eyes and get up.

The fragrance of this meditation will remain with you throughout the day.

THE NOVICE MONK

Mindfulness is being in the 'present'.

Forget the past and do not worry about the future. Be fully present, here, and now.

Enjoy the beautiful surroundings and savour the joys.

Dr Martin Seligman shares an interesting parable on mindfulness in his book on happiness:

"After three years of study, the novice monk arrives at the dwelling of his teacher. He enters the room, bursting with ideas about knotty issues of Buddhist metaphysics, and well-prepared for the deep questions that await him in his examination.

"I have but one question," his teacher intones.

"I am ready, master," he replies.

"In the doorway, were the flowers to the left or to the right of the umbrella?"

"The novice retires, abashed, for three more years of study."

FLOW

Have you seen a musician playing music? She becomes so engrossed in the activity that she becomes oblivious of the surroundings. As time elapses, she becomes one with the musical instrument. There is no musician and no musical instrument. Only music!

This is what is known as optimal experience. Such a state is known as the state of flow.

All creative pursuits lead to a state of flow.

Activities like music, dance, sports, and games are conducive for experiencing flow.

You may also experience flow while reading an absorbing book, watching a rainbow, or even at work.

ARBEJDSGLAEDE

Happiness at work? Seems strange, but it is true.

They have a word in the Danish language – arbejdsglaede.

Arbejde means work and *glaede* means happiness. *Arbejdsglaede* literally translates into work-happiness.

Happiness at work is a feeling derived from work.

Alexander Kjerulf is the author of a lovely book with the title 'Happy hour is 9 to 5'. In the book, he elaborates:

"Happiness at work is a feeling you get when you:

Really enjoy what you do,

Do great work you can feel proud of,

Work with amazing people,

Know that what you do is important,

Are appreciated for your work,

Get to take responsibility,

Have fun at work,

Learn and grow,

Make a difference,

Are motivated and energized,

Know that you kick butt."

The experience of flow makes our life richer, more complex, and intense.

To experience flow, find an activity that you find interesting, that you love to do, that gives you a sense of satisfaction and fulfilment.

Do it with full concentration and absorption. Go deeper and deeper into it.

Engage fully to meet the challenges the task offers by upscaling your skills by continuous learning. Find ways and means to repeat the activity again and again.

BEAUTIFUL DAY

Positive psychology is the modern science of happiness. They have created a rich repertoire of happiness activities.

These activities are evidence based and scientifically tested.Dr Martin Seligman describes one such activity:

"Set aside a free day every month to indulge in your favourite pleasures.

"Pamper yourself.

Have a beautiful day.

"Design, in writing, what you will do from hour to hour.

"Be mindful and savour every moment of the beautiful day.

"Do not let the bustle of life interfere and carry out the plan."

THREE BLESSINGS

This is another happiness activity from positive psychology. It is also called the WHAT-WENT-WELL exercise.

It can be incorporated into your daily routine without spending any extra time.

The exercise as described in positive psychology goes like this:

"Each night before going to sleep, write down three things that went well during the day, that made you happy or things for which you are grateful.

"These may be small things or important ones.

"Doing this exercise regularly can help you appreciate the positive in your life rather than take it for granted."

You can do this exercise on our own or with a loved one - a partner, child, parent, sibling, or close friend.

Expressing gratitude together can contribute in a meaningful way to the relationship.

LAUGHTER
MEDITATION

Laughter and meditation seem to be contrary to each other. Laughter is full of activity and movement, while meditation requires stillness and calm.

Laughter meditation is a blissful experience. It is especially suitable for those who find it difficult to practice other forms of meditation.

When you laugh, you forget the past. You cannot bother about the future. And you are oblivious of the surroundings. Laughter starts to flow like a fountain.

There is no *laugher*, it is only laughter. The laugher mingles with laughter and they become one.

It is something divine. It is pure and pristine bliss. The mind becomes serene and radiant like the full moon.

Laughter meditation may be experienced while

standing up, sitting down, or lying.

Just close your eyes and start laughing gently.
Let laughter take its own course.
If you do not feel like laughing, stop.
When you again feel like laughing, laugh.
After you have laughed for a while, relax.
Open your eyes.

BEAUTIFUL MIND

Whether you live in Dharavi or at the Beverly Hills is immaterial, if you have a beautiful mind.

A beautiful mind ideally dwells in the four heavenly abodes: Loving kindness, compassion, sympathetic joy, and equanimity.

These are also known as the four sublime states of mind, or the *Brahma viharas* – abode of the Brahma.

One must develop love and kindness for all sentient beings, compassion for those in need, altruistic joy in the success of others, and equanimous attitude under all circumstances.

These four states are sublime because they are the right attitude, the ideal way of conduct towards living beings.

The four sublime states remove all tensions. They make peace in social conflict.

These sublime states can be developed through *metta* meditation – a practice of wishing well for all beings.

They should become the mind's constant dwelling-places. They should become those places in the mind where we feel *at home*.

The four sublime states should become our inseparable companions, and we should be mindful of them in all our everyday common activities.

HAPPINESS
MANTRA

Do yoga and meditation every morning or go for a walk in the park and exercise.

Smile and be kind to all.

Spend quality time with family and friends.

Engage deeply in work, study, play, love, and parenting.

Connect with a meaningful cause.

BORN TO BE HAPPY

We are all born to be happy but, somehow, people live their lives in storybook fashion, unwilling to experience their own uniqueness.

The purpose of this book is to show simple ways that can change the course of your life.

It is based on the premise that you can create your own happiness. This is supported by the modern science of happiness as well as ancient spirituality.

THE PARABLE OF THE EAGLE

Have you heard of the parable of the eagle?

It is paraphrased excellently by Muriel James and Dorothy Jongeward in 'Born to win':

"Once upon a time, while walking through the forest, a certain man found a young eagle. He took it home and put it in his barn-yard where it soon learned to eat chicken feed and to behave as chickens behave.

"One day, a naturalist who was passing by inquired of the owner why it was that an eagle, the king of all birds, should be confined to live in the barnyard with the chickens.

"Since I have given it chicken feed and trained it to be a chicken, it has never learned to fly," replied the owner. "It behaves as chickens behave, so it is no longer an eagle."

"Still," insisted the naturalist, "it has the heart of an eagle and can surely be taught to fly."

"After talking it over, the two men agreed to find out whether this was possible. Gently the naturalist took the eagle in his arms and said, "You belong to the sky, and not to the earth. Stretch forth your wings and fly."

"The eagle, however, was confused; he did not know who he was, and, seeing the chickens eating their food, he jumped down to be with them again.

"Undismayed, the naturalist took the eagle on the following day, up on the roof of the house, and urged him again, saying, "You are an eagle. Stretch forth your wings and fly." But the eagle was afraid of his unknown self and world and jumped down once more for the chicken food.

"On the third day the naturalist rose early and took the eagle out of the barnyard to a high mountain. There, he held the king of birds high above him and encouraged again, saying, "You are an eagle. You belong to the sky as well as to the earth. Stretch forth your wings now, and fly."

"The eagle looked around, back towards the barnyard and up to the sky. Still, he did not fly. Then the naturalist lifted him straight towards the sun and it happened that the eagle began to tremble, slowly he stretched his wings. At last, with a triumphant cry, he soared into the heavens.

"It may be that the eagle still remembers the chickens with nostalgia; it may be that he occasionally revisits the barnyard. But as far as anyone knows, he has never returned to lead the life of a chicken, He was an eagle though he had been kept and tamed as a chicken."

Just like the eagle, people who earlier accepted unhappiness as their fate, can experience new happiness and freedom. The sky is the limit.

Never forget, you can create your own happiness by taking care of your mind and body, heart and soul.

Be happy and stay blessed!

ABOUT THE AUTHOR

Jagat Singh Bisht

Author, Blogger, Laughter Yoga Master Trainer, Founder: Life-Skills, Behavioural Science Trainer, and National Science Talent Scholar.

He is a Laughter Yoga Master Trainer of international repute and has been propagating happiness and well-being among people for the past twenty years.

He served in a bank for thirty-five years and has published five books, including 'CULTIVATING HAPPINESS: A GUIDE TO PRACTICES THAT DO WONDERS'.

Printed in Great Britain
by Amazon